STREAMLINING SUCCESS:
Global Business Services for Human Resources (HR), Digital Marketing (DM), and Management (MT) in SMEs

SEBASTIAN RÖMISCHER

Content

Content
Introduction
Acknowledgments
About the Author
Foreword

Chapter 1
The Evolution of Global Business Services
Understanding Global Business Services
The Importance of GBS in SMEs
Trends Shaping the Future of GBS

Chapter 2
Revolutionizing Human Resources
Redefining HR Functions in SMEs
Leveraging Technology for HR Efficiency
Building a Global Talent Pipeline

Chapter 3
Digital Marketing Strategies for Success
The Digital Landscape: Opportunities and Challenges
Crafting a Winning Digital Marketing Plan
Measuring Success: Key Performance Indicators

Chapter 4
Management Excellence through Global Services
The Role of Management in Global Operations
Strategies for Effective Leadership in SMEs
Fostering a Culture of Continuous Improvement

Chapter 5
Integrating HR, Marketing, and Management
The Synergy Between HR and Marketing
Collaborative Management for Optimal Results

Case Studies: Successful Integration in SMEs

Chapter 6
Overcoming Challenges in Global Business Services
Identifying Common Pitfalls
Strategies for Risk Management
Adapting to Change: Flexibility in Operations

Chapter 7
The Future of SMEs in a Globalized World
Embracing Innovation and Technology
Sustainability and Social Responsibility
Preparing for the Next Generation of Business

Chapter 8
Actionable Steps for SMEs and StartUps
Developing a Strategic Roadmap
Building a Resilient Business Model
Creating a Network of Support and Resources

Chapter 9
Inspiring Success Stories
Interviews with SME Leaders
Learning from Failures and Triumphs
The Power of Community and Collaboration

Chapter 10
Conclusion - Your Path to Streamlined Success
Reflecting on Key Insights
Taking Action: Your Next Steps
Embracing the Journey Ahead
Your Path to Streamlined Success

Introduction

Welcome to "Streamlining Success: Global Business Services for Human Resources, Digital Marketing, and Management in SMEs." In an era where small and medium-sized enterprises (SMEs) face unprecedented challenges and opportunities, the need for effective strategies and streamlined processes has never been more critical. This book aims to provide you with a comprehensive understanding of Global Business Services (GBS) and how they can be leveraged to enhance operational efficiency, drive growth, and foster innovation within your organization.

As we navigate through the chapters, you will discover insights into the evolution of GBS, the revolutionizing of human resources, effective digital marketing strategies, and management excellence. Each section is designed to equip you with actionable tools and frameworks that can be tailored to your unique business context. Whether you are an entrepreneur looking to launch a startup or a seasoned leader seeking to optimize existing operations, this book offers valuable guidance on integrating HR, marketing, and management functions for optimal results.

My journey in personal and professional development has shaped my understanding of what it takes to succeed in today's dynamic business environment. With over 20 years of experience in this field, I have dedicated my career to empowering individuals and organizations alike. Together, let us embark on this journey toward streamlined success.

Acknowledgments

I would like to take this opportunity to express my heartfelt gratitude to everyone who has contributed to the creation of this book. First and foremost, I want to thank my family for their unwavering support and encouragement throughout my journey. Your belief in me has been a constant source of motivation.

I am also deeply grateful to my mentors and colleagues who have shared their wisdom and insights over the years. Your guidance has enriched my understanding of personal and professional development, allowing me to better serve those around me. A special thanks goes out to the many individuals I have had the privilege of coaching and mentoring; your stories of growth and transformation inspire me every day.

To the teams I have collaborated with in various organizations—thank you for your trust in my expertise. Your commitment to embracing change has made it possible for us to achieve remarkable results together. I also want to acknowledge the incredible community in Moldova that welcomed me when I emigrated from Germany over a decade ago; your warmth and resilience have profoundly impacted my life.

Lastly, I extend my appreciation to all readers who embark on this journey with me. It is my hope that the insights shared within these pages will empower you as you strive for success in your own endeavors.

About the Author

Hello, my name is Sebastian Römischer, and I bring over 20 years of experience in personal and professional development. More than a decade ago, I made the life-changing decision to emigrate from Germany to the Republic of Moldova. Since then, I have dedicated myself to using my energy and knowledge to support over 10,000 individuals in discovering their true calling and abilities.

As a certified trainer, coach, and mentor from SGD® Darmstadt, I specialize in various topics including personal development, self- and time management, stress management, positive thinking, life coaching, business coaching, and mentoring. Additionally, as a certified hypnotherapist from TMI® Darmstadt, I offer life coaching training alongside mental coaching services.

My expertise extends into meditation practices, relaxation techniques, and autogenic training according to Schultz's methods. Having personally experienced burnout myself, I understand how energy and commitment can serve as catalysts for significant change. Through my Life-Business-System© approach, I provide an efficient framework for realizing desires while fostering sustainable revenue growth.

With extensive knowledge in digital marketing and business development strategies at hand, I've assisted numerous companies in strengthening their online presence while increasing revenues through effective marketing initiatives. Furthermore, I support businesses in streamlining processes through tailored solutions within Business Process Outsourcing (BPO).

By combining these diverse skills into holistic solutions aimed at sustainable growth and development for businesses across sectors - let's work together towards shaping your path toward success!

Foreword

In today's fast-paced and interconnected world, small and medium-sized enterprises (SMEs) and startups face a myriad of challenges that can often feel overwhelming. The need for efficiency, adaptability, and strategic insight has never been more crucial. This subchapter serves as a roadmap, guiding these businesses through the transformative potential of global business services tailored specifically for Human Resources (HR), Digital Marketing (DM), and Management (MT). By tapping into these services, SMEs can streamline operations, enhance their competitive edge, and foster sustainable growth, all while maintaining their unique vision and values.

The first section will delve into the realm of Human Resources, illuminating how strategic outsourcing can revolutionize the way SMEs manage their workforce. From recruitment to compliance, HR processes can be complex and time-consuming. By leveraging global business services, SMEs can access a wealth of expertise and technology that not only simplifies these tasks but also enriches the employee experience. This chapter will explore innovative HR solutions that empower organizations to attract top talent, cultivate a thriving workplace culture, and ensure compliance with ever-evolving regulations, ultimately transforming HR into a strategic partner in business success.

Next, we will explore the dynamic landscape of Digital Marketing, a critical component for SMEs aiming to carve out their niche in the global marketplace. The digital realm offers unprecedented opportunities for engagement and growth, but navigating this space can be daunting. This section will outline how global business services can provide SMEs with the tools and insights needed to elevate their marketing strategies. From data analytics to content creation and social media management, these services enable startups to amplify their brand presence, connect authentically with their audience, and drive measurable results. By harnessing the power of digital marketing, SMEs can transcend geographical boundaries and establish themselves as leaders in their respective fields.

The final segment will focus on Management, emphasizing the importance of effective leadership and strategic planning in fostering resilience and innovation. For SMEs, the ability to adapt quickly to market changes is vital. This chapter will highlight how global business services can facilitate the implementation of best practices in management, from project management to financial oversight. By adopting these services, SMEs can enhance their operational efficiency, make data-driven decisions, and respond proactively to emerging challenges. This section aims to inspire SMEs to view management not just as a necessity, but as a catalyst for creativity and growth, enabling them to thrive in an increasingly competitive landscape.

In conclusion, "Streamlining Success: Global Business Services for HR, Marketing, and Management in SMEs" is more than just a guide; it's an invitation to embrace a future where SMEs can harness the power of global services to achieve extraordinary outcomes. By integrating innovative HR practices, dynamic digital marketing strategies, and effective management solutions, businesses can streamline their operations and foster a culture of continuous improvement. This subchapter aims to inspire SMEs and startups to envision a future where success is not just attainable but inevitable, encouraging them to take bold steps toward transforming their aspirations into reality.

Chapter 1
The Evolution of Global Business Services

Understanding Global Business Services

In the rapidly evolving landscape of business, understanding Global Business Services (GBS) is essential for SMEs and StartUps aiming to thrive in a competitive world. GBS encompasses a wide range of centralized services that can significantly enhance operational efficiency, reduce costs, and foster innovation. By leveraging GBS, small and medium-sized enterprises can harness the power of global resources, ensuring that they not only survive but thrive in an interconnected market. The journey toward integrating GBS into your operations is not merely a strategic move; it is a transformative step towards achieving greater agility and responsiveness to market demands.

At its core, GBS involves consolidating functions such as Human Resources, Digital Marketing, and Management under a unified framework. This integration allows businesses to streamline processes, eliminate redundancies, and create a more focused approach to service delivery. For SMEs, this means gaining access to world-class expertise without the overhead costs typically associated with large-scale operations. By centralizing these functions, businesses can harness data analytics for better decision-making, foster collaboration across departments, and ultimately enhance the employee and customer experience. The potential for increased productivity and innovation is boundless, empowering SMEs to compete on a global scale.

Human Resources is one of the most critical areas where GBS can make a substantial impact. By adopting a global perspective, SMEs can access a diverse talent pool, implement standardized processes, and enhance employee engagement and retention. The ability to manage HR functions such as recruitment, training, and performance management from a centralized platform not only saves time but also ensures consistency in policies and practices. This centralized approach enables businesses to focus on building a strong organizational culture while adapting to the unique needs of a global workforce, ultimately driving long-term success.

Digital Marketing, too, stands to benefit immensely from the GBS model. In a world where online presence is paramount, SMEs must adopt a cohesive digital strategy that resonates with global audiences. By centralizing digital marketing efforts, businesses can create a unified brand voice, leverage cutting-edge analytics, and implement targeted campaigns that drive engagement and conversion. GBS in digital marketing allows SMEs to pool resources, share insights, and develop innovative strategies that can be scaled across different markets. This approach not only maximizes marketing effectiveness but also fosters a culture of creativity and collaboration, essential for navigating the complexities of today's digital landscape.

Finally, the realm of Management is where the visionary potential of GBS truly shines. By embracing a global service framework, SMEs can enhance their strategic planning, operational efficiency, and overall governance. This holistic approach empowers leaders to make informed decisions backed by data and insights gathered from various functions. The collaborative environment fostered by GBS encourages innovation and agility, enabling SMEs to pivot swiftly in response to market changes. As businesses embark on this journey, they unlock new avenues for growth and success, transforming challenges into opportunities that pave the way for a brighter future. Embracing Global Business Services is not just a strategy; it is a commitment to excellence and a bold step towards realizing the full potential of your enterprise.

The Importance of GBS in SMEs

The rise of global business services (GBS) has transformed the landscape for small and medium-sized enterprises (SMEs), illuminating pathways to efficiency and growth that were once the exclusive domain of larger corporations. In today's interconnected world, SMEs and startups are no longer confined to local markets; they are empowered to compete on a global scale. The importance of GBS lies not just in its ability to streamline operations, but in its potential to unlock new avenues for innovation, collaboration, and market expansion. As SMEs embrace GBS, they position themselves at the forefront of their industries, ready to seize opportunities that can lead to unprecedented success.

At the core of GBS is the unification of business functions, which allows SMEs to consolidate their operations across various domains, including human resources, digital marketing, and management. This consolidation does not merely simplify processes; it fosters a culture of synergy and collaboration. By integrating HR and marketing services, for instance, businesses can attract top talent while simultaneously enhancing their brand presence. The ability to streamline these functions enables SMEs to allocate resources more effectively, ensuring that every team member is aligned with the company's overarching goals. This alignment not only drives productivity but also cultivates an environment where innovation flourishes, setting the stage for sustainable growth.

Moreover, GBS empowers SMEs to leverage data analytics, a critical component in today's digital landscape. With access to real-time insights, businesses can make informed decisions that propel them ahead of the competition. For instance, through integrated marketing services, companies can analyze consumer behavior and preferences, allowing them to tailor their offerings with precision. Similarly, in HR, data-driven strategies can enhance talent acquisition and retention, ensuring that SMEs attract and keep the best employees. By harnessing the power of data, SMEs can adapt quickly to market changes and customer needs, fostering resilience and agility in an ever-evolving business environment.

The role of GBS in promoting cost efficiency cannot be overstated. For many SMEs, operating within tight budgets is a reality that demands innovative solutions. GBS allows for the creation of shared services that reduce duplication and lower operational costs. By centralizing functions such as payroll processing or digital marketing campaigns, SMEs can benefit from economies of scale, directing more resources towards strategic initiatives rather than routine tasks. This financial prudence is essential for startups looking to establish a foothold in competitive markets, allowing them to invest in growth opportunities that drive long-term success.

Finally, embracing GBS is not just a strategic decision; it is a commitment to the future of the business. As the global marketplace continues to evolve, SMEs must be willing to adapt and innovate. By integrating GBS into their operations, these enterprises position themselves as agile players ready to navigate the complexities of international business. The importance of GBS in SMEs extends beyond operational improvement; it embodies a shift in mindset that champions collaboration, efficiency, and a relentless pursuit of excellence. In doing so, SMEs can not only survive but thrive, paving the way for a bright and prosperous future in the global economy.

Trends Shaping the Future of GBS

As the landscape of Global Business Services (GBS) continues to evolve, it's imperative for SMEs and startups to remain attuned to the trends shaping the future of this dynamic field. The convergence of technology, globalization, and changing workforce expectations is not just transforming operations; it's redefining the very essence of how businesses connect, engage, and thrive in a competitive marketplace. Embracing these trends will empower organizations to streamline their processes, enhance their service delivery, and ultimately achieve greater success.

One of the most significant trends influencing GBS is the integration of advanced technologies such as artificial intelligence (AI) and automation. These tools are no longer the future; they are the present, revolutionizing HR, digital marketing, and management practices. For SMEs and startups, leveraging AI can lead to more efficient recruitment processes, personalized marketing strategies, and data-driven decision-making. By automating routine tasks, organizations can refocus their human resources on strategic initiatives that drive growth and innovation. The ability to harness technology effectively is a transformative opportunity, allowing smaller businesses to compete on a global scale.

Another key trend is the rise of remote and hybrid work models. The COVID-19 pandemic accelerated a shift that was already underway, prompting businesses to rethink their operational frameworks. For SMEs, this transition opens doors to a broader talent pool, enabling access to diverse skills and perspectives without geographic limitations. Embracing flexible work arrangements not only enhances employee satisfaction but also fosters a culture of inclusivity and adaptability. As businesses navigate this new normal, prioritizing employee well-being and engagement will be essential in attracting and retaining top talent.

Sustainability and social responsibility are also becoming central to GBS strategies. Today's consumers and employees are increasingly conscious of the societal impact of their choices. SMEs that prioritize ethical practices and sustainable operations will not only build trust with their stakeholders but also differentiate themselves in the marketplace. Integrating sustainability into HR policies, marketing campaigns, and management strategies is not just a trend; it's a pathway to building a resilient business that resonates with modern values. Organizations that lead with purpose will inspire loyalty and foster long-term relationships with customers and employees alike.

Finally, the importance of data analytics in decision-making cannot be overstated. As GBS increasingly relies on insights derived from data, SMEs must cultivate a data-driven culture that informs every aspect of their operations. From understanding customer behavior in digital marketing to optimizing HR processes and enhancing management strategies, data analytics provides the clarity needed to make informed choices. By investing in analytical capabilities, SMEs can unlock new opportunities, identify emerging trends, and navigate challenges with confidence, ensuring sustained growth in a rapidly changing environment.

In conclusion, the future of Global Business Services is being shaped by technological advancements, evolving work models, a commitment to sustainability, and the power of data analytics. For SMEs and startups, embracing these trends is not just a strategic advantage; it's an invitation to innovate and excel in a global marketplace. By staying ahead of the curve and integrating these elements into their core operations, businesses can streamline their success and secure a brighter future. The journey may be challenging, but the rewards of resilience, adaptability, and visionary thinking are boundless.

Chapter 2
Revolutionizing Human Resources

Redefining HR Functions in SMEs

In the dynamic landscape of small and medium-sized enterprises (SMEs), the traditional functions of Human Resources (HR) are being challenged and transformed. As organizations strive to remain competitive in a global marketplace, the role of HR is evolving beyond administrative tasks and compliance checks. It is becoming a strategic partner that not only drives the organization's culture but also enhances employee engagement and aligns human capital with business objectives. For SMEs and startups, this transformation is not just beneficial; it is essential for thriving in an ever-changing environment.

At the heart of redefining HR functions is the recognition that people are an organization's greatest asset. In SMEs, where resources may be limited, leveraging talent effectively can lead to remarkable innovation and growth. By adopting a holistic approach to HR, organizations can create a robust framework that fosters an inclusive workplace culture, encourages continuous learning, and prioritizes employee well-being. This new paradigm shifts the focus from merely filling positions to building a talented workforce that is motivated, empowered, and aligned with the company's vision.

Technology plays a pivotal role in this transformation. With the advent of digital tools and platforms, HR functions can be streamlined, making processes more efficient and data-driven. From recruitment to performance management, leveraging technology allows SMEs to optimize their HR operations. For instance, utilizing Applicant Tracking Systems (ATS) can significantly enhance the recruitment process by automating candidate screenings and improving the quality of hires. Furthermore, data analytics can provide insights into employee performance and engagement, enabling HR professionals to make informed decisions that drive organizational success.

Moreover, redefining HR functions in SMEs involves fostering a culture of adaptability and resilience. In a world where change is constant, organizations must embed flexibility into their HR practices. This means embracing remote work, offering flexible schedules, and creating a culture that values innovation and experimentation. By empowering employees to take ownership of their roles and encouraging them to contribute ideas, SMEs can cultivate an environment where creativity thrives, leading to enhanced problem-solving and a competitive edge in the market.

Ultimately, the redefinition of HR functions in SMEs signifies a shift towards a more strategic and people-centric approach. As startups and small businesses navigate the complexities of the global market, prioritizing the human element can unlock tremendous potential. By investing in their workforce and embracing innovative HR practices, SMEs can not only streamline their operations but also inspire a culture of excellence that propels them toward sustained success. In this journey, HR emerges as a catalyst for change, driving organizations toward their goals while creating a fulfilling and engaging workplace for all.

Leveraging Technology for HR Efficiency

In today's fast-paced business landscape, small and medium-sized enterprises (SMEs) and startups face unique challenges in managing human resources effectively. Leveraging technology for HR efficiency is not merely an option; it is a necessity that can pave the way for sustainable growth and success. By embracing innovative tools and solutions, businesses can streamline their HR processes, reduce administrative burdens, and focus on what truly matters: nurturing talent and driving engagement.

The advent of digital platforms has transformed the traditional HR landscape. Cloud-based solutions enable SMEs to manage recruitment, onboarding, performance evaluations, and employee engagement with unprecedented ease. This shift allows HR professionals to transition from time-consuming administrative tasks to strategic decision-making roles. By automating routine processes such as payroll and attendance tracking, organizations can significantly reduce errors and free up valuable time that can be redirected towards employee training and development initiatives.

Data analytics plays a pivotal role in enhancing HR efficiency. By harnessing the power of data, SMEs can gain insightful perspectives into their workforce dynamics. Predictive analytics can identify trends related to employee performance, turnover, and satisfaction, enabling businesses to make informed decisions. This data-driven approach not only enhances the overall employee experience but also aligns HR strategies with broader organizational goals. When SMEs leverage technology to interpret and act on workforce data, they position themselves to foster a culture of continuous improvement and adaptability.

Moreover, technology fosters a more inclusive and engaging workplace. Virtual collaboration tools and communication platforms bridge geographical gaps, allowing SMEs to tap into global talent pools. By implementing flexible work arrangements and remote onboarding processes, organizations can attract diverse candidates from various backgrounds. This inclusivity not only enriches the workplace culture but also drives innovation and creativity, essential ingredients for success in today's competitive market. Technology empowers SMEs to create a vibrant and dynamic environment where every employee feels valued and motivated to contribute.

In conclusion, the journey toward HR efficiency through technology is one of empowerment and transformation. SMEs and startups that embrace these advancements will not only optimize their HR functions but also cultivate a resilient workforce ready to tackle future challenges. By investing in the right technology, organizations can unlock the full potential of their human capital, driving engagement and performance. The time to leverage technology is now; doing so will pave the way for lasting success in the ever-evolving landscape of global business services.

Building a Global Talent Pipeline

Building a global talent pipeline is crucial for SMEs and startups aiming to compete in an increasingly interconnected world. As businesses expand their operations beyond domestic borders, the need for diverse and skilled talent becomes paramount. A well-structured talent pipeline can significantly enhance an organization's capacity to innovate, adapt, and thrive in global markets. By viewing talent acquisition through a global lens, SMEs can access a wealth of skills and perspectives that drive growth and foster creativity.

The first step in building a global talent pipeline is to define your organization's unique value proposition. What makes your company an attractive place for top talent? Understanding your brand identity and what sets you apart in the marketplace is essential. SMEs often have the advantage of agility and a dynamic work environment, which can be appealing to prospective employees. Leveraging this identity in your recruitment strategy not only attracts talent but also cultivates a sense of belonging among employees, encouraging them to contribute to the company's mission and vision.

Once your value proposition is established, the next phase involves strategic sourcing of talent. This means identifying the regions and markets where the skills you need are abundant. Utilizing digital platforms and professional networks can connect you with potential candidates worldwide. Additionally, collaborating with local recruitment agencies or educational institutions can provide insights into emerging talent pools. By casting a wide net, SMEs can discover diverse candidates who bring fresh ideas and unique perspectives, essential for fostering innovation and driving business success.

Moreover, technology plays a pivotal role in building a global talent pipeline. Investing in human resource management systems and digital recruitment tools can streamline the hiring process, making it easier to track candidates, manage applications, and communicate effectively across different time zones. Virtual interview platforms and assessment tools ensure that you can evaluate candidates based on their skills and fit without geographical constraints. Embracing technology not only improves efficiency but also enhances the candidate experience, making your organization more appealing to top talent.

Finally, nurturing your global talent pipeline requires commitment to ongoing training and development. Once you have attracted the right talent, it's vital to invest in their growth through mentorship programs, workshops, and continuous education. Creating a culture of learning not only retains employees but also empowers them to contribute meaningfully to your organization. As SMEs and startups cultivate their global talent pipeline, they position themselves to adapt to market changes and seize new opportunities, ultimately leading to long-term success in the global marketplace.

Chapter 3
Digital Marketing Strategies for Success

The Digital Landscape: Opportunities and Challenges

The digital landscape has transformed the way small and medium-sized enterprises (SMEs) and startups operate, offering unprecedented opportunities alongside distinct challenges. As we navigate this dynamic environment, businesses must recognize that embracing digital transformation is not merely an option; it is a necessity for survival and growth. In the realms of Human Resources, Digital Marketing, and Management, the integration of technology can streamline processes, enhance engagement, and ultimately drive success. By leveraging these tools, SMEs can position themselves to compete on a global scale while fostering innovation and agility.

In Human Resources, the digital revolution has redefined the way organizations attract, retain, and develop talent. With sophisticated software solutions, SMEs can automate routine tasks such as payroll processing and employee onboarding, freeing HR professionals to focus on strategic initiatives that foster a positive workplace culture. Moreover, digital platforms enable companies to tap into global talent pools, allowing them to find the best candidates regardless of geographical constraints. By harnessing data analytics, businesses can gain insights into employee performance and engagement, paving the way for targeted interventions that enhance productivity and job satisfaction.

Digital Marketing presents an equally exciting frontier for SMEs and startups. The rise of social media, content marketing, and search engine optimization offers businesses the tools to engage customers directly and build lasting relationships. In this environment, SMEs can compete with larger corporations by leveraging creative, cost-effective marketing strategies that resonate with their target audience. The ability to analyze consumer behavior in real time means that businesses can adapt their strategies quickly, ensuring they remain relevant and responsive to market changes. This agility not only enhances brand reputation but also drives customer loyalty, a critical component for long-term success.

However, the digital landscape is not without its challenges. The rapid pace of technological advancement can create a sense of overwhelm, particularly for SMEs with limited resources. Implementing new systems can require significant investment in both time and money, and the risk of data breaches poses a constant threat in an increasingly interconnected world. Moreover, the digital divide means that not all businesses have equal access to technology, potentially exacerbating existing inequalities. To thrive in this environment, SMEs must cultivate a mindset of continuous learning and adaptability, embracing change as an integral part of their growth journey.

Ultimately, the digital landscape is a double-edged sword that offers both opportunities and challenges for SMEs and startups. By recognizing the potential of digital tools in Human Resources, Digital Marketing, and Management while remaining aware of the hurdles they must overcome, businesses can create a roadmap for success. Embracing innovation, fostering a culture of adaptability, and investing in the right technology will enable SMEs to not only survive but thrive in this ever-evolving digital world. The journey may be fraught with uncertainties, but with courage and vision, the potential for success is limitless.

Crafting a Winning Digital Marketing Plan

Crafting a winning digital marketing plan is a crucial step for SMEs and startups aiming to carve out their space in an increasingly competitive global landscape. In an era where digital presence is paramount, a well-structured marketing strategy can propel a business from obscurity to prominence. The journey begins with understanding the unique needs of your target audience. By conducting thorough market research and identifying buyer personas, businesses can tailor their messaging and offerings to resonate deeply with potential customers. This foundational step not only ensures that marketing efforts are focused but also establishes a connection that fosters loyalty and trust.

Next, setting clear, measurable objectives is essential for guiding your digital marketing efforts. These objectives should align with your overall business goals, whether it's increasing brand awareness, boosting sales, or enhancing customer engagement. By employing the SMART criteria—Specific, Measurable, Achievable, Relevant, and Time-bound—businesses can create a roadmap that is both ambitious and feasible. This clarity not only motivates teams but also makes it easier to track progress and adjust strategies as needed. Remember, flexibility is key in digital marketing; the landscape is ever-changing, and a willingness to adapt can be the difference between success and stagnation.

Integrating diverse digital channels is another critical component of a successful marketing plan. From social media platforms that engage audiences to email marketing campaigns that nurture leads, each channel offers unique opportunities to connect with potential customers. A multichannel approach not only broadens your reach but also reinforces your brand message across various touchpoints. Consider leveraging content marketing to provide valuable information that addresses your audience's pain points. This not only positions your brand as an authority in your field but also fosters a sense of community among your customers, encouraging them to share and engage with your content.

Moreover, utilizing analytics tools to measure the effectiveness of your digital marketing efforts allows for data-driven decision-making. By analyzing metrics such as website traffic, conversion rates, and customer engagement, businesses can gain valuable insights into what strategies are working and which need refinement. This continuous feedback loop empowers SMEs to optimize their campaigns, allocate resources more effectively, and ultimately enhance their return on investment. The beauty of digital marketing lies in its ability to provide real-time data, enabling businesses to pivot quickly and stay ahead of the competition.

Finally, cultivating a culture of innovation within your organization can significantly enhance your digital marketing efforts. Encouraging creative brainstorming sessions and fostering collaboration among team members can lead to fresh ideas and unique approaches to reaching your audience. Embrace experimentation and don't shy away from trying new tactics, whether it's exploring emerging social media platforms or adopting cutting-edge marketing technologies. In the fast-paced world of digital marketing, those who dare to innovate and adapt will not only survive but thrive, paving the way for sustained success and growth in the global marketplace.

Measuring Success: Key Performance Indicators

Measuring success is essential for any SME or startup striving to navigate the complexities of global business services in human resources, digital marketing, and management. Key performance indicators (KPIs) serve as the vital metrics that provide insight into organizational performance and help you gauge the effectiveness of your strategies. By establishing clear and measurable KPIs, you empower your team to focus on what truly matters, creating a culture of accountability and continuous improvement. In this journey, understanding how to define, track, and analyze these indicators will not only illuminate your path to success but also inspire your team to reach new heights.

In the realm of human resources, KPIs such as employee retention rates and time-to-hire can provide invaluable insights into your organization's health. These metrics help you assess whether your recruitment strategies are effective and if employees are satisfied in their roles. For SMEs and startups, a strong focus on talent management can foster a motivated workforce that contributes to business growth. By regularly reviewing these indicators, you can adapt your HR practices, ensuring that your team remains engaged and aligned with your company's objectives. Remember, the heart of any successful business lies in its people, and understanding their needs through KPIs can make all the difference.

Digital marketing is another critical area where KPIs can illuminate the effectiveness of your campaigns. Metrics such as conversion rates, customer acquisition cost, and return on investment (ROI) are pivotal in determining whether your marketing efforts are resonating with your audience. For SMEs and startups, leveraging these indicators allows for agile decision-making and the ability to pivot strategies in real-time. Establishing a data-driven marketing approach will not only enhance customer engagement but also ensure that your resources are allocated efficiently. By celebrating small victories reflected in your KPIs, you can motivate your team and encourage a culture of innovation and experimentation.

Management practices also benefit significantly from well-defined KPIs. Metrics like project completion rates, budget adherence, and employee productivity can provide a comprehensive view of operational efficiency. For small and medium-sized enterprises, having a clear understanding of these indicators helps in identifying bottlenecks and optimizing processes. Regularly analyzing these metrics allows managers to make informed decisions that drive performance, ultimately leading to sustainable growth. When management is transparent about performance expectations and celebrates achievements, it fosters a positive environment where every team member feels valued and empowered to contribute.

In conclusion, measuring success through key performance indicators is not just a task but a transformative journey for SMEs and startups. By embracing a culture that prioritizes data-driven insights across human resources, digital marketing, and management, you position your organization for long-term success. These metrics are not merely numbers; they represent the collective efforts of your team and serve as a roadmap towards achieving your business goals. As you embark on this path, remember that every small improvement, guided by these indicators, can lead to significant breakthroughs in your quest for success. Embrace the journey, celebrate progress, and watch your organization thrive.

Chapter 4
Management Excellence through Global Services

The Role of Management in Global Operations

The landscape of global business is ever-evolving, presenting both challenges and opportunities for small and medium-sized enterprises (SMEs) and startups. In this dynamic environment, the role of management in global operations is not merely a function of oversight but a strategic catalyst for success. Management must navigate the complexities of diverse markets, cultures, and regulatory frameworks, ensuring that global operations align with the organization's vision and goals. By fostering a culture of agility and adaptability, management can empower teams to thrive in varied environments, ultimately streamlining success across international borders.

At the heart of effective management in global operations lies the necessity for a clear and inspiring vision. Leaders must articulate a compelling purpose that resonates with their teams, transcending geographical and cultural boundaries. This vision serves as a guiding light, motivating employees to embrace challenges and pursue excellence. In the domain of human resources, for instance, management plays a pivotal role in cultivating a workforce that is not only skilled but also culturally aware and engaged. By investing in training and development, management can unlock the potential of a diverse talent pool, creating a workforce that is ready to tackle the demands of a global marketplace.

Digital marketing, an essential component of global operations, requires management to adopt innovative strategies that leverage technology and data analytics. Managers must harness the power of digital platforms to engage with customers across the globe, tailoring marketing efforts to meet local preferences while maintaining a cohesive brand identity. This dual focus on localization and global consistency is crucial. Management must encourage experimentation and creativity within marketing teams, fostering an environment where bold ideas can flourish. As a result, SMEs and startups can build strong international brands that resonate with their target audiences.

In the realm of management, effective communication is paramount. As teams span different time zones and cultures, management must establish clear communication channels that promote collaboration and transparency. Utilizing technology to facilitate virtual meetings, project management tools, and instant messaging platforms is essential for maintaining connectivity. Moreover, management should prioritize building relationships based on trust and mutual respect, recognizing that a cohesive team is more likely to overcome obstacles and achieve shared objectives. This culture of open dialogue not only enhances operational efficiency but also nurtures an environment where innovation can thrive.

Ultimately, the role of management in global operations is about more than just overseeing tasks—it's about inspiring a collective journey toward success. By embracing a visionary approach, investing in talent development, leveraging digital marketing strategies, and fostering effective communication, management can create a robust framework for growth. SMEs and startups that prioritize these elements will not only navigate the complexities of global business with confidence but also position themselves as leaders in their industries. In this interconnected world, the potential for success is limitless, and with the right management strategies in place, every organization can reach new heights.

Strategies for Effective Leadership in SMEs

In the dynamic landscape of Small and Medium Enterprises (SMEs) and startups, effective leadership stands as a cornerstone of success. The ability to inspire teams, navigate challenges, and implement strategic initiatives can elevate an organization from mere survival to thriving. For leaders in SMEs, particularly in the realms of Human Resources, Digital Marketing, and Management, the emphasis should be on cultivating a vision that resonates throughout the organization. By fostering a culture of inclusivity and innovation, leaders can empower their teams to explore new horizons while ensuring that every voice is heard.

One of the primary strategies for effective leadership lies in the art of communication. Clear, transparent communication fosters trust and collaboration among team members. Leaders should prioritize open dialogues, encouraging feedback that can lead to innovative solutions. In a world where digital communication is prevalent, the challenge is to maintain personal connections. Regular team meetings, brainstorming sessions, and one-on-one check-ins can enhance relational dynamics, allowing leaders to tap into the collective intelligence of their teams. This approach not only nurtures engagement but also cultivates an environment where creativity flourishes.

Adaptability is another critical trait that effective leaders must embody. The fast-paced nature of SMEs requires leaders to remain agile and responsive to market changes. This means being willing to pivot strategies and embrace new technologies that can streamline processes and enhance productivity. Leaders should encourage a culture of experimentation, where team members feel safe to test new ideas without fear of failure. By promoting a mindset of learning and resilience, leaders can drive their organizations forward, positioning them to seize opportunities that others may overlook.

Empowerment is equally vital in effective leadership. By delegating responsibilities and trusting team members to take ownership of their roles, leaders can foster a sense of accountability and pride within the workforce. This empowerment leads to higher levels of motivation and job satisfaction, which are crucial for retaining top talent in the competitive landscape of SMEs. Additionally, providing opportunities for professional development through training and mentorship can help individuals grow their skills and prepare for greater challenges, ultimately benefiting the organization as a whole.

Finally, visionary leadership involves a commitment to long-term goals that align with the core values of the organization. Leaders must articulate a clear vision that inspires their teams to work towards a common purpose. This vision should be rooted in a deep understanding of the market and the unique value proposition of the organization. By integrating sustainable practices and embracing social responsibility, leaders can position their SMEs as not only profitable entities but also as contributors to the greater good. This holistic approach to leadership not only drives business success but also creates a lasting legacy that resonates beyond the confines of the organization. Through these strategies, leaders can steer their SMEs towards a future of innovation, collaboration, and excellence.

Fostering a Culture of Continuous Improvement

Fostering a culture of continuous improvement is not just a strategic initiative; it is a mindset that transforms the way small and medium enterprises (SMEs) operate. In the dynamic landscape of global business services, particularly within the realms of Human Resources, Digital Marketing, and Management, the ability to adapt and evolve is a hallmark of successful organizations. For SMEs and startups, cultivating this culture means embracing change, encouraging innovation, and recognizing that every team member plays a pivotal role in the journey toward excellence. This shift in perspective can unlock untapped potential, driving growth and resilience.

Continuous improvement begins with a commitment to learning. In the context of HR, this could mean re-evaluating recruitment strategies to attract diverse talent, fostering an inclusive workplace, or implementing feedback mechanisms that empower employees. By creating opportunities for professional development and encouraging employees to share their insights, SMEs can innovate their processes and enhance employee engagement. This commitment not only attracts top talent but also cultivates a workforce that is aligned with the organization's goals, ultimately leading to improved productivity and morale.

In the realm of digital marketing, continuous improvement yields significant competitive advantages. The digital landscape evolves rapidly; therefore, staying ahead requires a proactive approach. SMEs can foster a culture of experimentation, where teams are encouraged to test new strategies, analyze their effectiveness, and iterate based on data-driven insights. This iterative process not only enhances marketing campaigns but also fosters creativity and collaboration. By leveraging analytics and embracing a fail-forward mentality, organizations can refine their strategies and deliver more value to their customers.

Management practices, too, benefit immensely from a culture of continuous improvement. Leaders in SMEs must model behaviors that prioritize adaptability and open communication. This means seeking feedback from employees at all levels, recognizing achievements, and addressing challenges transparently. When leaders actively engage with their teams and demonstrate a willingness to adjust plans based on collective input, they create an environment where innovation thrives. This sense of shared purpose fosters loyalty and motivates employees to take ownership of their contributions, driving the organization toward its strategic objectives.

Ultimately, fostering a culture of continuous improvement is about building a resilient organization that embraces change as a catalyst for growth. For SMEs and startups, the journey may be challenging, but the rewards are profound. By embedding this culture into the fabric of the organization, leaders not only enhance operational efficiency but also inspire their teams to strive for excellence. As businesses navigate the complexities of global markets, the commitment to continuous improvement will be the cornerstone of sustainable success, propelling SMEs to new heights in the ever-evolving landscape of HR, Digital Marketing, and Management.

Chapter 5
Integrating HR, Marketing, and Management

The Synergy Between HR and Marketing

The synergy between Human Resources (HR) and Marketing is a powerful alliance that can propel small and medium-sized enterprises (SMEs) and startups toward unprecedented success. In today's competitive landscape, the barriers between these two essential functions are increasingly blurred, creating opportunities for innovative collaboration that can enhance brand identity, employee engagement, and overall organizational performance. By fostering a culture where HR and Marketing work hand-in-hand, businesses can effectively align their internal and external messaging, creating a cohesive narrative that resonates with both employees and customers.

One of the most compelling aspects of this synergy is the potential for shared storytelling. HR plays a vital role in shaping the company's culture, values, and vision, while Marketing is tasked with communicating these elements to the outside world. When these departments collaborate, they can craft authentic and engaging narratives that reflect the organization's true essence. This alignment not only strengthens the employer brand but also attracts talent that aligns with the company's values, ensuring that the workforce is as passionate about the organization's mission as its customers are. Ultimately, a unified narrative empowers SMEs to build an authentic brand that stands out in a crowded marketplace.

Moreover, the integration of HR and Marketing can significantly enhance employee engagement and retention. Marketing strategies that focus on employer branding can showcase the company as an attractive workplace, highlighting employee stories, achievements, and positive experiences. HR can leverage these marketing initiatives to create targeted recruitment campaigns that resonate with prospective employees. By presenting a compelling image of the workplace and fostering a sense of belonging, SMEs can cultivate a loyal workforce that is more likely to contribute to the company's success. This holistic approach not only reduces turnover rates but also boosts productivity, as employees feel more connected to their roles and the overall mission of the organization.

Additionally, the collaboration between HR and Marketing opens up avenues for innovative employee training and development programs. Marketing professionals are adept at understanding consumer behavior and market trends, insights that can be invaluable in shaping training initiatives that resonate with employees. By utilizing marketing analytics, HR can identify skill gaps and tailor training programs that not only enhance employee capabilities but also align with the organization's strategic goals. This proactive approach to talent development not only equips the workforce with the necessary skills but also fosters a culture of continuous improvement and learning, positioning SMEs for sustainable growth.

In conclusion, the synergy between HR and Marketing is not just a beneficial partnership; it is a strategic imperative for SMEs and startups striving for success in a global marketplace. By embracing collaboration, organizations can create a compelling narrative that attracts top talent, enhances employee engagement, and drives overall performance. As these two functions work together, they can cultivate a vibrant organizational culture that not only meets the needs of the business but also inspires employees and customers alike. In an era where authenticity and connection are paramount, the alignment of HR and Marketing is a powerful catalyst for achieving streamlined success in the dynamic world of global business services.

Collaborative Management for Optimal Results

In today's rapidly evolving business landscape, the power of collaborative management cannot be overstated, especially for small and medium-sized enterprises (SMEs) and startups. As organizations strive to optimize their resources and enhance their competitive edge, embracing a collaborative approach can lead to remarkable results. By fostering an environment where ideas and expertise can flourish harmoniously, SMEs can tap into the collective intelligence of their teams, driving innovation and efficiency across Human Resources, Digital Marketing, and Management.

At the heart of collaborative management is the belief that every team member has something valuable to contribute. In the realm of Human Resources, this means leveraging diverse perspectives to create a more inclusive workplace. By encouraging open communication and collaboration among employees, HR leaders can identify the unique strengths and weaknesses of their workforce. This not only enhances employee engagement but also cultivates a culture of continuous improvement. When team members feel valued and heard, they are more likely to contribute their best efforts, resulting in a motivated and high-performing organization.

In the domain of Digital Marketing, collaboration facilitates the sharing of insights and strategies that can significantly elevate a brand's presence in a crowded marketplace. By bringing together individuals with varying skill sets—ranging from content creators to data analysts—marketing teams can develop comprehensive campaigns that resonate with their target audience. Collaboration allows for brainstorming sessions that ignite creativity and pave the way for innovative marketing solutions. As SMEs harness the power of teamwork in their digital marketing efforts, they not only enhance their brand visibility but also foster a sense of unity and purpose within their teams.

Effective management practices in SMEs also benefit immensely from a collaborative approach. By engaging employees in decision-making processes, leaders can cultivate a sense of ownership and accountability. This empowerment encourages team members to take initiative and propose solutions to challenges, fostering a proactive organizational culture. Additionally, collaborative management ensures that different departments work seamlessly together, breaking down silos that often hinder productivity. When HR, marketing, and management teams collaborate, they can align their goals and strategies, creating a cohesive vision that propels the entire organization forward.

Ultimately, the journey toward optimal results through collaborative management is one of shared responsibility and mutual growth. For SMEs and startups, the willingness to embrace collaboration can unlock untapped potential and drive sustainable success. By prioritizing collaboration across all facets of the organization, leaders can inspire their teams to innovate, adapt, and thrive in an ever-changing business environment. As we move forward, let us recognize that the collective strength of our teams is the key to not just surviving, but flourishing in the global business landscape.

Case Studies: Successful Integration in SMEs

In the rapidly evolving landscape of global business services, small and medium-sized enterprises (SMEs) and startups are uniquely positioned to harness the transformative power of strategic integration. This subchapter explores inspiring case studies that exemplify successful integration in the realms of Human Resources, Digital Marketing, and Management. These stories not only showcase best practices but also illuminate the paths these organizations took to streamline their operations, enhance their competitive edge, and drive sustainable growth.

One remarkable case is that of a mid-sized software development firm that faced challenges in talent acquisition and employee retention. By adopting a comprehensive human resources information system (HRIS), the organization automated its recruitment process, enabling it to attract top talent from around the globe. This integration not only reduced the time-to-hire significantly but also provided valuable analytics that informed strategic decisions regarding employee engagement and development. The impact was profound: the company reported a 30% increase in employee satisfaction and a 25% decrease in turnover rates, demonstrating that when SMEs invest in robust HR processes, they can build a resilient workforce poised for innovation.

In the realm of digital marketing, a small boutique agency exemplified the power of integrating data-driven strategies into its operations. Initially overwhelmed by the vast amounts of data generated from various campaigns, the agency implemented a cohesive marketing automation platform that streamlined its efforts across multiple channels. By centralizing its data and utilizing advanced analytics, the agency was able to tailor its messaging, optimize its ad spend, and significantly enhance customer engagement. As a result, the agency not only doubled its client base within a year but also increased its revenue by 40%, proving that thoughtful integration can lead to explosive growth in the competitive digital landscape.

Management integration also plays a crucial role in the success of SMEs. A family-owned manufacturing business faced stagnation due to outdated management practices and a lack of strategic direction. By embracing modern management methodologies, including agile frameworks and collaborative tools, the company revitalized its operations. The leadership involved employees at all levels in the decision-making process, fostering a culture of innovation and accountability. This shift led to increased productivity, with project turnaround times reduced by 50%. The company's journey illustrates how effective management integration not only optimizes operational efficiency but also cultivates a dynamic workplace where every employee feels valued.

These case studies serve as powerful reminders that successful integration is not solely the domain of large corporations. SMEs and startups, with their agility and innovative spirit, can achieve remarkable outcomes by embracing global business services in HR, digital marketing, and management. The experiences of these organizations highlight the importance of adaptability, data-driven decision-making, and a commitment to employee engagement. As the landscape of business continues to evolve, the stories of these SMEs stand as beacons of inspiration, encouraging others to embark on their own journeys toward streamlined success.

Chapter 6
Overcoming Challenges in Global Business Services

Identifying Common Pitfalls

Identifying common pitfalls is essential for SMEs and startups seeking to thrive in the competitive landscape of global business services. Understanding these obstacles empowers organizations to circumvent potential setbacks and fosters resilience and adaptability. In the realms of Human Resources, Digital Marketing, and Management, the journey is often fraught with challenges that can derail even the most well-intentioned initiatives. By shining a light on these pitfalls, businesses can transform obstacles into opportunities for innovation and growth.

One of the most prevalent pitfalls in HR is the failure to align talent acquisition with the company's strategic goals. Many SMEs invest significant resources in hiring but neglect to consider how new roles will contribute to long-term objectives. This misalignment can lead to a workforce that lacks cohesion and direction. To avoid this trap, businesses should develop a clear understanding of their vision and ensure that every hiring decision supports it. By fostering a culture of alignment, organizations not only attract the right talent but also cultivate an engaged workforce that is motivated to drive success.

In the realm of digital marketing, a common misstep lies in the overemphasis on technology at the expense of genuine customer engagement. While tools and platforms can enhance outreach, they cannot replace the human element that resonates with audiences. SMEs often get caught up in metrics and data analytics, losing sight of the importance of storytelling and authentic connections. To navigate this pitfall, businesses must prioritize building relationships with their customers, leveraging technology as a means to enhance, rather than replace, human interaction. An approach that balances technology with empathy can lead to deeper brand loyalty and customer satisfaction.

Management practices within SMEs are not immune to pitfalls either, particularly regarding communication and collaboration. In fast-paced environments, leaders may inadvertently overlook the importance of fostering open dialogue among team members. This can result in silos, where departments operate in isolation, stifling creativity and innovation. To combat this issue, leaders should champion a culture of transparency and inclusivity, encouraging feedback and collaboration across all levels. By breaking down barriers and nurturing a collaborative atmosphere, organizations can unlock the collective potential of their teams and propel their success.

Lastly, the challenge of scalability often haunts SMEs as they strive for growth. Many businesses fall into the trap of sticking with processes that worked in the early stages but are ill-suited for expansion. This resistance to change can hinder progress and stifle innovation. To avoid this pitfall, organizations must be willing to reassess and adapt their strategies continually. Embracing a mindset of agility allows businesses to pivot when necessary and seize new opportunities. By fostering a culture that values continuous improvement, SMEs can position themselves for sustainable growth in an ever-evolving market.

Identifying common pitfalls is not merely about recognizing what can go wrong; it is about cultivating a proactive approach to business strategy. For SMEs and startups, awareness of these challenges can serve as a catalyst for innovation, guiding them toward a path of resilience and success in global business services. By learning from the experiences of others and remaining adaptable, organizations can confidently navigate the complexities of HR, Digital Marketing, and Management, turning potential setbacks into stepping stones toward achieving their vision.

Strategies for Risk Management

In an ever-evolving global landscape, small and medium-sized enterprises (SMEs) and startups face a myriad of challenges that can jeopardize their growth and sustainability. Risk management is no longer a luxury but a fundamental necessity that can turn potential threats into opportunities for innovation and resilience. As you embark on your journey in the domains of Human Resources, Digital Marketing, and Management, embracing effective risk management strategies is essential in navigating uncertainties and achieving streamlined success.

The first strategy lies in cultivating a proactive mindset towards risk identification. By fostering a culture of awareness within your organization, you empower your team to recognize potential risks before they escalate. Encourage open dialogue and brainstorming sessions where employees can voice concerns and insights. Utilizing tools such as risk assessment matrices can help visualize potential threats across various operational domains. This proactive approach not only mitigates risks but also enhances team engagement and collaboration, creating a unified front against challenges.

Once potential risks are identified, the next step is prioritization. Not all risks carry the same weight; some may have a more direct impact on your business than others. Implementing a scoring system based on factors such as likelihood and potential impact can aid in determining which risks require immediate attention and resources. For SMEs and startups, focusing on the most pressing risks allows for more strategic allocation of limited resources, ensuring that your energy is spent on areas that directly affect your bottom line.

In the dynamic fields of HR, Digital Marketing, and Management, technology plays a crucial role in risk management. Leverage data analytics and digital tools to monitor market trends, customer behavior, and employee satisfaction. By harnessing real-time data, you can anticipate shifts in the business environment and make informed decisions that mitigate risks. Additionally, investing in cybersecurity measures protects sensitive company and client information, safeguarding your brand's reputation and trustworthiness. In this digital age, technology is not just an enabler; it is a powerful ally in your risk management arsenal.

Moreover, fostering strong relationships with stakeholders is vital in building a resilient business framework. Engage with your clients, suppliers, and employees, creating an environment where feedback is valued and acted upon. Open communication channels allow for the identification of potential risks that may not be immediately visible. Collaborating with other SMEs and startups can also provide insights into shared challenges and collective solutions. By building a supportive network, you create a safety net that can cushion the impact of unforeseen risks.

Lastly, adaptability is the cornerstone of effective risk management. The ability to pivot in response to changing circumstances can mean the difference between thriving and merely surviving. Encourage a culture of learning and flexibility within your organization, where team members are empowered to embrace change and think creatively. Regularly review and update your risk management strategies to align with evolving business goals and market conditions. By fostering an agile mindset, your SME or startup will not only withstand risks but will also transform them into catalysts for growth and innovation, propelling your journey toward sustained success.

Adapting to Change: Flexibility in Operations

Adapting to change is not merely a strategic choice; it is an essential cornerstone for the survival and growth of small and medium-sized enterprises (SMEs) and startups in today's dynamic landscape. In a world that is constantly shifting due to technological advancements, evolving consumer preferences, and economic fluctuations, the ability to pivot and embrace flexibility in operations can spell the difference between stagnation and thriving success. For those engaged in global business services, particularly in Human Resources, Digital Marketing, and Management, fostering a culture that encourages adaptability is not just beneficial; it is imperative.

Flexibility in operations begins with a mindset shift. Leaders and team members must cultivate an environment where innovation is celebrated, and change is seen as an opportunity rather than a threat. Embracing this mindset allows SMEs to respond swiftly to market demands and align their strategies with emerging trends. In Human Resources, for example, this could mean adopting new technologies that streamline recruitment processes or implementing flexible work arrangements that cater to the evolving needs of employees. Such adaptability not only enhances operational efficiency but also fosters a sense of trust and collaboration within teams.

In the realm of Digital Marketing, flexibility is equally vital. The digital landscape is ever-changing, driven by algorithms, social media trends, and consumer behavior shifts. SMEs must be agile enough to adjust their marketing strategies in real time, harnessing data analytics to identify what resonates with their audience. This could involve pivoting from one platform to another or experimenting with new content formats to better engage potential customers. By embracing a culture of experimentation and rapid iteration, businesses can discover what works best, allowing them to optimize their marketing efforts continuously.

Management practices also benefit immensely from a flexible approach. As teams become more diverse and global, the traditional top-down management style may no longer be effective. Instead, fostering a collaborative environment where feedback is encouraged and decisions are made collectively can lead to innovative solutions and improved morale. Utilizing agile project management methodologies, for instance, enables teams to adapt to changing project requirements without losing momentum. This flexibility not only enhances productivity but also empowers employees, making them feel valued and invested in the company's success.

Ultimately, the journey of adapting to change is not a solitary endeavor; it requires a collective commitment from every member of the organization. SMEs and startups that embrace flexibility in their operations stand to gain a competitive edge in an ever-evolving marketplace. By fostering a culture of adaptability, organizations can enhance their resilience, innovate continually, and navigate the complexities of global business services with confidence. In a world that thrives on change, those who remain flexible will not only survive but flourish, turning challenges into opportunities for growth and success.

Chapter 7
The Future of SMEs in a Globalized World

Embracing Innovation and Technology

In an era defined by rapid technological advancements, small and medium-sized enterprises (SMEs) and startups stand at a pivotal crossroads. The ability to embrace innovation and technology is not just a competitive advantage; it is a necessity for survival and growth in today's global business landscape. As businesses navigate the complexities of human resources, digital marketing, and management, leveraging innovative solutions can streamline operations, enhance productivity, and foster a culture of creativity. By actively seeking out and integrating new technologies, SMEs can position themselves as leaders in their respective fields, inspiring not only their teams but also their customers and stakeholders.

The integration of cutting-edge tools in human resources can transform the way SMEs attract, develop, and retain talent. Traditional HR practices often fall short in addressing the unique challenges faced by smaller businesses. However, by adopting innovative HR technologies—such as artificial intelligence for recruitment, performance management tools, and employee engagement platforms—SMEs can create a more dynamic and responsive workplace. These technologies not only simplify administrative processes but also empower employees, allowing them to contribute to their fullest potential. When HR functions are streamlined and efficient, organizations can focus on their core mission, fostering growth and innovation throughout the company.

In the realm of digital marketing, the landscape is evolving at an unprecedented pace. With the rise of social media, data analytics, and personalized marketing, SMEs have the opportunity to reach wider audiences and engage with customers in more meaningful ways. Embracing innovation in digital marketing means leveraging these tools to craft compelling narratives that resonate with target audiences. By utilizing data-driven insights, businesses can tailor their marketing strategies, ensuring that their messages are not only heard but also felt. This personalized approach fosters loyalty and trust, essential ingredients for long-term success in a crowded marketplace.

Management practices, too, are undergoing a transformation fueled by technology. Agile methodologies, remote collaboration tools, and project management software are redefining how teams operate and communicate. For SMEs and startups, embracing these innovations can lead to enhanced efficiency and collaboration. By adopting a culture of continuous improvement, organizations can harness the collective intelligence of their teams, driving innovation from within. Leaders who prioritize technological integration and encourage adaptability create an environment where creativity thrives, ensuring that their businesses remain relevant and competitive in a rapidly changing world.

Ultimately, embracing innovation and technology is about more than just adopting the latest tools; it is about fostering a mindset that values growth and adaptability. For SMEs and startups, this shift can unlock new opportunities, drive operational excellence, and enhance the overall employee and customer experience. As the global business landscape continues to evolve, those who are willing to innovate and embrace change will not only survive but thrive. By inspiring a culture that values innovation, SMEs can chart a course toward sustained success, leaving a lasting impact on their industries and communities.

Sustainability and Social Responsibility

Sustainability and social responsibility are not just buzzwords; they are fundamental pillars that define the modern business landscape, especially for SMEs and startups. As organizations strive to carve their niche in competitive markets, the integration of sustainable practices and a commitment to social responsibility can set them apart. This approach not only resonates with consumers who increasingly favor brands that align with their values but also fosters a workplace culture that attracts top talent. By weaving sustainability into the fabric of their operations, SMEs can cultivate a brand identity that is both principled and profitable.

In the realm of Human Resources, sustainability and social responsibility manifest in the way organizations treat their employees and communities. A commitment to equitable hiring practices, employee well-being, and diversity creates a more engaged workforce. Businesses that prioritize these values are not merely fulfilling a moral obligation; they are enhancing their reputation and performance. HR leaders can champion initiatives that promote a healthy work-life balance, support mental health, and encourage professional development, reinforcing the notion that employee satisfaction is integral to long-term success.

Digital Marketing serves as a powerful vehicle for communicating sustainability efforts and social responsibility initiatives. In a world where consumers are inundated with messages, authenticity stands out. SMEs that transparently share their sustainability journey—be it through eco-friendly practices, charitable partnerships, or community engagement—can build trust and loyalty. Digital platforms enable companies to tell their stories effectively, showcasing their commitment to making a positive impact. This not only attracts like-minded customers but also invites partnerships with other organizations that share similar values, creating a ripple effect of positive change.

Management practices, too, must reflect a commitment to sustainability and social responsibility. Leaders in SMEs and startups have the unique opportunity to implement strategies that prioritize ethical decision-making and responsible resource management. This includes everything from reducing waste and optimizing supply chains to fostering a culture of innovation that encourages sustainable solutions. By embedding these principles into their core strategies, leaders can drive not only financial performance but also contribute to a healthier planet and society.

Ultimately, embracing sustainability and social responsibility is not just about compliance or improving the bottom line; it is about envisioning a future where businesses thrive alongside their communities and the environment. SMEs and startups that take bold steps toward integrating these values will not only position themselves for success in an increasingly conscientious market but also inspire others to follow suit. As they embark on this journey, they contribute to a legacy of positive impact, proving that responsible business practices are not just good ethics—they are good business.

Preparing for the Next Generation of Business

As the landscape of global business continues to evolve, small and medium-sized enterprises (SMEs) and startups stand at a pivotal crossroads. The surge in technological advancements, shifting consumer behaviors, and an increasingly competitive marketplace necessitate a proactive approach to business strategy. This subchapter aims to inspire leaders in HR, digital marketing, and management to embrace a forward-thinking mindset. By preparing for the next generation of business, they can ensure sustainable growth and foster innovation that resonates with the demands of the modern world.

At the heart of this preparation lies the need for agility. Businesses that thrive in the current climate are those that can adapt swiftly to changes. SMEs must cultivate a culture that encourages flexibility and embraces change as a constant. This could mean re-evaluating traditional HR practices to adopt more dynamic recruitment strategies or leveraging data analytics in digital marketing to tailor campaigns to individual customer preferences. By instilling an agile mindset, organizations can not only respond more effectively to market fluctuations but can also anticipate trends and position themselves as industry leaders.

Moreover, collaboration and integration across departments are essential in streamlining success. Human resources, marketing, and management must work hand-in-hand to create a cohesive strategy that aligns with the overall vision of the company. For instance, HR can play a crucial role in shaping the organizational culture that supports innovative marketing efforts, while management can provide the strategic direction needed for both functions to flourish. By fostering an environment of collaboration, SMEs can harness the collective strengths of their teams, leading to enhanced productivity and creativity.

Investing in technology is another critical component in preparing for the future. The rapid advancement of digital tools presents an opportunity for SMEs to optimize their operations and engage more effectively with their customers. From AI-driven recruitment platforms in HR to automated marketing solutions that enhance customer engagement, the right technology can drive efficiency and scalability. However, it's not merely about adopting the latest tools; it's about understanding how these technologies can be integrated into the existing business framework to create value and enhance the customer experience.

Finally, the journey towards preparing for the next generation of business is an ongoing one. It requires a commitment to continuous learning and a willingness to innovate. Leaders must be open to new ideas, seek feedback from their teams, and invest in their own professional development. By fostering a culture of learning and curiosity, SMEs and startups can equip themselves to navigate the complexities of the global business environment. As they embrace this journey, they will not only prepare for the challenges ahead but will also inspire their teams to reach new heights, ultimately paving the way for a successful and sustainable future.

Chapter 8
Actionable Steps for SMEs and StartUps

Developing a Strategic Roadmap

Developing a Strategic Roadmap is a pivotal step for small and medium-sized enterprises (SMEs) and startups seeking to thrive in the competitive landscape of global business services. In the realms of Human Resources, Digital Marketing, and Management, a well-crafted roadmap serves as both a guiding star and a practical tool, illuminating the path toward operational excellence. It empowers organizations to align their goals, streamline processes, and harness the potential of their workforce and technology. By embracing a strategic mindset, SMEs can not only navigate challenges but also seize opportunities that propel them toward success.

The first phase of developing a strategic roadmap begins with a clear understanding of the organization's vision and mission. Leaders must engage in introspective conversations, asking fundamental questions about the purpose of their business and the value they aim to provide to their customers. This foundational clarity fosters a sense of direction and purpose that is essential for rallying the team and stakeholders around common objectives. When everyone is aligned on the mission, it cultivates a culture of accountability and motivation, driving employees to contribute meaningfully to the organization's success.

Next, it is crucial to conduct a thorough analysis of the current state of the business. This involves assessing internal capabilities and external market conditions. For SMEs and startups, every insight gained can lead to powerful revelations about strengths to leverage and weaknesses to address. In the context of Human Resources, this might mean evaluating talent acquisition strategies or employee engagement initiatives. In Digital Marketing, it could involve analyzing current campaigns and market positioning. Management practices should also be scrutinized to identify inefficiencies that could be optimized. This comprehensive analysis lays the groundwork for informed decision-making and strategic prioritization.

With a solid understanding of the organization's vision and current landscape, the next step is to set measurable goals and define the strategies to achieve them. Goals should be ambitious yet attainable, inspiring teams to stretch their limits while remaining realistic about resource constraints. In HR, this could translate into initiatives aimed at enhancing employee skills and retention. For Digital Marketing, it may involve expanding reach through innovative campaigns. Management strategies might focus on optimizing operations or enhancing customer service. By establishing clear milestones, SMEs can track progress and celebrate achievements, fostering a culture of continuous improvement.

Finally, the effectiveness of a strategic roadmap hinges on its implementation and adaptability. It is essential to communicate the roadmap clearly to all team members, ensuring that everyone understands their role in the larger picture. Regular check-ins and reviews allow for adjustments based on real-time feedback and market dynamics. Embracing a mindset of flexibility ensures that SMEs can pivot when necessary, seizing new opportunities or addressing unforeseen challenges. By nurturing a culture of collaboration and innovation, organizations can build resilience and sustain growth, transforming their strategic roadmap into a living document that evolves alongside their ambitions. In this journey, the ability to adapt and innovate will ultimately define success in the ever-changing landscape of global business services.

Building a Resilient Business Model

Building a resilient business model is crucial for SMEs and startups navigating the ever-evolving landscape of global business services. With the rapid pace of technological advancements and changing market dynamics, having a business model that can withstand disruptions and adapt to new challenges will not only enhance sustainability but also encourage growth. This chapter aims to inspire you to rethink your strategies, embrace flexibility, and create a solid foundation that allows your organization to thrive, regardless of external pressures.

At the heart of a resilient business model lies a deep understanding of your core values and mission. This clarity serves as a guiding star for decision-making and helps in maintaining focus amid uncertainty. SMEs and startups should take the time to articulate their unique value propositions within the realms of HR, digital marketing, and management. By aligning business objectives with these values, organizations can foster a culture of adaptability and innovation. This alignment empowers teams to respond proactively to market changes, ultimately leading to a competitive edge that is both sustainable and impactful.

Collaboration is another vital aspect of building resilience in your business model. In an interconnected world, leveraging partnerships can open doors to new opportunities and resources. For SMEs and startups, forging alliances with other organizations, service providers, or even industry influencers can enhance capabilities and broaden market reach. Whether it's collaborating with a digital marketing agency for a joint campaign or partnering with an HR technology provider to streamline hiring processes, these relationships can significantly amplify your potential for success. Embrace the power of collaboration to create a network of support that strengthens your business model.

Technology plays a transformative role in fostering resilience. By integrating digital tools and platforms, SMEs can enhance operational efficiency, improve customer engagement, and make data-driven decisions. The adoption of cloud-based solutions, automation, and analytics can streamline HR processes, optimize marketing strategies, and facilitate effective management practices. These technological innovations not only improve productivity but also enable businesses to pivot quickly in response to changing market conditions. As you embrace these advancements, remember that technology should align with your business goals and values, reinforcing your overall resilience.

Finally, cultivating a culture of continuous learning and improvement is essential for a resilient business model.

Encourage your team to embrace change and seek out new knowledge, whether through training, workshops, or industry events. Foster an environment where experimentation is welcomed, and failures are seen as valuable learning experiences. This mindset not only empowers employees but also fuels creativity and innovation within your organization. By prioritizing growth and development, SMEs and startups can build a resilient business model that not only survives challenges but thrives in the face of them. As you embark on this journey, remember that resilience is not just a goal; it is a continuous process of evolution and adaptation that can lead to enduring success.

Creating a Network of Support and Resources

Creating a robust network of support and resources is crucial for small and medium enterprises (SMEs) and startups aiming to navigate the complexities of global business services. In the dynamic landscape of Human Resources, Digital Marketing, and Management, the right connections can open doors to invaluable insights, mentorship, and collaborative opportunities. By fostering relationships with industry peers, experts, and organizations, businesses can enhance their capabilities, streamline operations, and position themselves for sustained growth.

The first step in building a network is to identify key stakeholders within your industry. This includes not only direct competitors but also complementary businesses that can offer insights into shared challenges and solutions. Engaging in industry events, workshops, and seminars is an excellent way to meet like-minded professionals who understand the unique hurdles faced by SMEs and startups. As you expand your network, remember that every conversation is a chance to learn, exchange ideas, and potentially form partnerships that can elevate your business to new heights.

Leveraging online platforms can further enhance your networking efforts. Social media channels like LinkedIn offer a wealth of resources for connecting with industry leaders, joining relevant groups, and participating in discussions that deepen your understanding of current trends and best practices. Additionally, online forums and communities dedicated to HR, Digital Marketing, and Management provide a supportive environment where you can ask questions, share experiences, and gain insights from those who have walked a similar path. Embracing these digital tools ensures that your network is not limited by geographical boundaries, allowing for a truly global perspective.

Mentorship plays a pivotal role in nurturing your network. Seek out seasoned professionals who can offer guidance based on their experiences. A mentor can help you navigate the complexities of global business services, providing insights that can save you time and resources. As you build these relationships, be open to sharing your own knowledge and experiences, creating a reciprocal flow of information that benefits both parties. This culture of giving and receiving not only strengthens your network but also fosters a community of support that is essential for growth and innovation.

Finally, consider the importance of formalizing your network through structured collaborations and partnerships. This could involve co-hosting events, sharing resources, or developing joint marketing strategies. By aligning your goals with those of your network, you can create synergies that amplify your reach and impact. Remember, success in today's business environment is rarely a solo endeavor; it thrives on collaboration and shared resources. By actively engaging in a network of support, SMEs and startups can not only streamline their operations but also cultivate an ecosystem that propels them towards success in the global marketplace.

Chapter 9
Inspiring Success Stories

Interviews with SME Leaders

In the rapidly evolving landscape of global business services, small and medium-sized enterprises (SMEs) and startups find themselves at a unique crossroads. The insights and experiences of industry leaders can illuminate the path forward, offering invaluable lessons in navigating the complexities of human resources, digital marketing, and management. By engaging with these leaders, we not only gain perspective on their journeys but also glean actionable strategies that can empower our own organizations to thrive in an increasingly competitive marketplace.

One common thread among successful SME leaders is their unwavering commitment to fostering a culture of innovation and adaptability. In an interview with Maria Chen, the CEO of a burgeoning tech startup, she emphasized the importance of embracing change as a constant. "In today's world, if you're not evolving, you're falling behind," Maria stated. Her company has successfully integrated agile methodologies into its HR practices, allowing for more flexible talent management and a workforce that is both engaged and resilient. This adaptability has not only streamlined their operations but has also positioned them as a leader in their niche, demonstrating that a proactive approach to change can yield remarkable results.

Digital marketing is another area where SME leaders are harnessing their creativity to drive growth. John Patel, who heads a small but dynamic marketing agency, shared his insights on leveraging data-driven strategies to connect with customers. "Understanding your audience is the first step toward crafting compelling marketing narratives," he explained. By utilizing analytics tools and social media platforms, John's team has been able to hone in on customer preferences, enabling them to deliver personalized experiences that resonate. This approach not only enhances customer loyalty but also fosters a deeper connection between the brand and its audience, exemplifying the transformative power of effective digital marketing in the SME sector.

Management practices are equally crucial in fostering a thriving organizational culture. In her discussion, Samantha Reyes, a veteran manager in the hospitality industry, highlighted the significance of transparent communication and employee empowerment. "When team members feel valued and heard, they contribute more creatively and enthusiastically," she noted. Samantha's approach to management involves regular feedback loops and inclusive decision-making processes, which have cultivated a sense of ownership among her staff. This not only boosts morale but also drives productivity, proving that effective management is about more than just overseeing tasks; it's about nurturing talent and encouraging collaboration at every level.

As we draw insights from these SME leaders, it becomes clear that the pillars of success in global business services lie in innovation, customer engagement, and effective management practices. Their stories serve as a beacon, guiding us through the intricacies of HR, digital marketing, and management. By adopting these principles and learning from their experiences, SMEs and startups can not only navigate the challenges they face but also create a blueprint for sustainable growth and success in a globalized business environment. The journey may be demanding, but with the right insights, it is undoubtedly achievable.

Learning from Failures and Triumphs

Learning from failures and triumphs is a crucial aspect of growth for small and medium enterprises (SMEs) and startups, particularly in the dynamic landscape of global business services. Each setback and success carries invaluable lessons that can shape the future trajectory of a business. In the realms of Human Resources, Digital Marketing, and Management, the ability to analyze and adapt based on past experiences can set an organization apart from its competitors. Embracing both the highs and lows not only fosters resilience but also cultivates a culture of continuous improvement, essential for thriving in today's fast-paced environment.

Failures, while often daunting, serve as powerful teachers. They compel businesses to reassess strategies, question assumptions, and innovate in ways that may not have been considered otherwise. For instance, an HR initiative that fails to boost employee engagement can reveal underlying issues within the organizational culture. This insight paves the way for more effective employee relations strategies that truly resonate with the workforce. By reflecting on these moments, SMEs can transform obstacles into stepping stones, ensuring that each misstep is a precursor to greater understanding and enhanced performance.

On the other hand, triumphs—big and small—deserve equal recognition. Celebrating successes not only boosts morale but also reinforces effective practices that can be replicated in the future. A successful digital marketing campaign might signal the importance of understanding target audiences and leveraging data analytics to drive results. By documenting these wins, SMEs can create a repository of best practices that fuels innovation and inspires teams. This dual focus on both achievements and setbacks fosters a balanced perspective, encouraging organizations to persistently seek improvement in all facets of their operations.

Moreover, a culture that embraces learning from both failures and triumphs fosters a growth mindset among employees. When team members feel safe to share their experiences, whether they are failures or successes, the entire organization benefits from a rich tapestry of insights. This culture encourages collaboration and creativity, leading to innovative solutions that drive efficiency and effectiveness in HR, Digital Marketing, and Management. By cultivating an environment where learning is prioritized, SMEs can empower their workforce to view challenges as opportunities for growth, thus enhancing both individual and organizational performance.

In conclusion, the journey of an SME or startup is often marked by a series of learning experiences derived from both failures and successes. By actively engaging with these lessons, businesses can refine their strategies and practices in Human Resources, Digital Marketing, and Management. The path to success is rarely linear; it is filled with peaks and valleys that, when navigated wisely, lead to profound growth and transformation. Embracing this journey with an inspirational outlook enables SMEs to not only survive but thrive, turning every experience into a stepping stone toward enduring success.

The Power of Community and Collaboration

In today's interconnected world, the essence of success for small and medium enterprises (SMEs) and startups lies not just in innovation or efficiency, but in the strength of community and collaboration. These two pillars can transform a solitary venture into a thriving ecosystem where shared knowledge, resources, and experiences lead to exponential growth. When SMEs and startups harness the power of community, they tap into a wealth of insights that can elevate their strategies in HR, digital marketing, and management. The collective intelligence of a network can illuminate pathways that might remain hidden in isolation.

Collaboration fosters a culture of shared learning and mutual support. Within the realms of HR, digital marketing, and management, SMEs can benefit immensely from partnerships with other businesses and professionals. For instance, collaborative workshops can facilitate the exchange of best practices in talent acquisition, employee engagement, and retention strategies. By sharing successes and failures, businesses can craft more effective HR frameworks that resonate with their unique corporate cultures. This collaborative learning environment not only enhances individual business practices but also strengthens the overall community, creating a robust support system that encourages innovation.

In the digital marketing landscape, collaboration can be a game changer. SMEs often compete with larger corporations that have substantial marketing budgets. However, by banding together, startups can leverage collective resources for joint marketing campaigns, pool their social media presence, and share customer insights. This approach not only amplifies their reach but also fosters a sense of camaraderie among businesses facing similar challenges. By working together, they can create compelling narratives that resonate with their target audiences, showcasing the unique strengths of each participant while driving collective brand visibility.

Management practices also flourish in a collaborative environment. SMEs can benefit from mentorship programs that connect emerging leaders with seasoned professionals. This exchange of expertise and insights can empower the next generation of managers to navigate the complexities of organizational development and strategic planning. Collaborative management also encourages diverse perspectives, leading to more innovative solutions. When businesses prioritize collaboration, they cultivate a culture of inclusivity and shared responsibility, which can lead to enhanced employee morale and productivity.

Ultimately, the power of community and collaboration is a significant catalyst for success in the realm of global business services. SMEs and startups that recognize and embrace this power will not only enhance their operational strategies but also contribute to building a resilient entrepreneurial ecosystem. By supporting one another, sharing resources, and collaborating on initiatives, these businesses can create a ripple effect that extends far beyond their individual ambitions. In this vibrant network of collaboration, success is not merely an endpoint but a shared journey, where every victory is celebrated collectively, paving the way for a brighter future for all.

Chapter 10
Conclusion - Your Path to Streamlined Success

Reflecting on Key Insights

Reflecting on key insights gained from the journey of integrating Global Business Services (GBS) into Human Resources, Digital Marketing, and Management can ignite a transformative spark for SMEs and startups. These insights not only illuminate the path to operational efficiency but also empower organizations to harness the full potential of their resources. As we ponder these lessons, we uncover the essence of what it means to thrive in an interconnected world, where agility and innovation are paramount.

One of the most significant insights revolves around the importance of adaptability. In an era marked by rapid technological advancements and shifting market dynamics, SMEs must cultivate a culture that embraces change. This adaptability extends beyond mere responsiveness; it involves proactively seeking out new tools and methodologies that can streamline processes and enhance service delivery. By integrating GBS into their operations, businesses can create a nimble framework that allows for real-time adjustments, ensuring they remain competitive and relevant in an ever-evolving landscape.

Equally vital is the realization that collaboration is the cornerstone of success. In the domains of HR, Digital Marketing, and Management, cross-functional collaboration fosters an environment where diverse ideas flourish. GBS serves as a catalyst for this synergy, breaking down silos and promoting open communication among teams. By learning from each other and sharing insights, SMEs can leverage their collective strengths, driving innovation and enhancing the overall customer experience. This collaborative spirit not only boosts morale but also positions organizations to respond more effectively to client needs.

Moreover, the integration of GBS highlights the significance of data-driven decision-making. In today's digital age, access to real-time data is a game changer for SMEs. By harnessing analytics and insights, businesses can make informed decisions that lead to impactful outcomes. GBS provides the tools necessary to analyze trends, measure performance, and gain a deeper understanding of customer behavior. This insight empowers organizations to tailor their strategies, ensuring they are not only meeting market demands but also anticipating future needs.

Finally, the journey of embracing GBS in HR, Digital Marketing, and Management ultimately leads to a powerful revelation: the value of investing in people. At the heart of every successful organization lies its workforce. As SMEs streamline their operations, they must prioritize the development of their talent pool. Training and upskilling initiatives foster a sense of loyalty and engagement among employees, driving productivity and innovation. By recognizing that people are the true asset of any business, organizations can cultivate a thriving culture that propels them toward long-term success.

In summary, reflecting on these key insights reveals a roadmap for SMEs and startups looking to harness the power of Global Business Services. By embracing adaptability, fostering collaboration, leveraging data, and investing in talent, businesses can not only streamline their operations but also unlock their full potential. As the world of business continues to evolve, those who embrace these principles will find themselves not just surviving, but thriving in the dynamic landscape of global commerce.

Taking Action: Your Next Steps

Taking action is the pivotal moment that transforms ideas into reality. For SMEs and startups navigating the complex landscape of global business services in HR, digital marketing, and management, the next steps are not merely tactical; they are strategic leaps toward sustainable success. As you stand at the crossroads of opportunity, remember that every great achievement begins with a single decision to move forward. Embrace this moment with confidence, knowing that the path you choose can shape the future of your organization.

Begin by assessing your current operations and identifying areas ripe for improvement. In the realm of human resources, this may involve evaluating your recruitment processes, employee engagement strategies, or even your compliance with global regulations. For digital marketing, consider the effectiveness of your online presence, the clarity of your messaging, and the engagement levels of your target audience. In management, analyze your decision-making processes and how effectively you are harnessing data to inform those decisions. This reflective practice will not only highlight areas needing attention but will also set a foundation for your action plan.

Next, prioritize your initiatives based on potential impact and feasibility. Focusing on high-impact changes will yield the most significant results with the resources you have available. For instance, improving your HR processes can lead to better talent acquisition, which directly affects your business's growth trajectory. Similarly, enhancing your digital marketing efforts could amplify your brand's visibility and customer engagement, creating a ripple effect that boosts sales and market share. Management improvements, such as adopting agile methodologies, can foster a culture of innovation and responsiveness to market changes. By concentrating your efforts on these high-impact areas, you create a powerful momentum that drives your organization forward.

As you embark on these initiatives, cultivate a culture of accountability and collaboration within your team. Encourage open communication and foster an environment where team members feel empowered to share ideas and feedback. This collaborative spirit not only enhances the quality of your strategies but also improves buy-in from your employees, making them more invested in the success of the initiatives. Regular check-ins and progress assessments will help maintain focus and ensure that everyone remains aligned with the overall vision. Remember, success is not a solitary journey; it thrives in a community that supports and inspires one another.

Finally, remain adaptable and open to learning throughout this process. The landscape of global business services is dynamic, and the ability to pivot in response to new challenges and opportunities will be crucial for your success. Regularly review your strategies and be willing to iterate based on what you learn. This mindset of continuous improvement will not only help you navigate obstacles but also position your SME or startup as a resilient player in the global market. Taking action is just the beginning; the journey of growth and success is an ongoing adventure that requires dedication, agility, and a commitment to excellence. Embrace it wholeheartedly, and watch your aspirations become achievements.

Embracing the Journey Ahead

As SMEs and startups navigate the complexities of today's global marketplace, the path to success is often filled with challenges and opportunities. The journey ahead is not merely about achieving targets or meeting deadlines; it is about fostering a culture of resilience, innovation, and adaptability. By embracing this journey, businesses can transform obstacles into stepping stones, cultivating a mindset that thrives on growth and progress. The world of global business services, particularly in HR, digital marketing, and management, offers an array of resources and strategies to help enterprises not only survive but flourish in this dynamic landscape.

The role of Human Resources in this journey cannot be overstated. HR is the backbone of every organization, serving as the bridge that connects talent with opportunity. In a global environment, attracting and retaining top talent requires a fresh perspective. Embracing the journey means investing in people, creating inclusive and diverse workplaces, and equipping teams with the tools they need to succeed. By adopting innovative HR practices, SMEs can enhance employee engagement and create a culture where individuals are empowered to contribute their best, driving the organization forward with collective strength.

Digital marketing is another vital component of this journey. As the digital landscape continues to evolve, businesses must be willing to adapt and reinvent their strategies. The power of storytelling, data analytics, and social media cannot be overlooked. Embracing the journey ahead involves leveraging these tools to connect with audiences in meaningful ways. By understanding customer needs and preferences, SMEs can craft tailored marketing campaigns that resonate on a global scale. This adaptability not only enhances brand visibility but also fosters lasting relationships with clients, ensuring sustained growth and relevance in an ever-changing market.

Management practices within SMEs must also evolve to meet the demands of a global audience. Embracing the journey ahead means embracing agility and innovation in leadership. Traditional management styles may no longer suffice in a world where change is the only constant. Forward-thinking leaders must cultivate a mindset that embraces experimentation, encourages collaboration, and values diverse perspectives. By fostering an environment where ideas can flourish, SMEs can stay ahead of the curve, responding swiftly to market shifts and positioning themselves as industry leaders.

Ultimately, the journey ahead is a shared experience, one that requires unity and collaboration across all levels of an organization. By embracing the potential of global business services in HR, digital marketing, and management, SMEs and startups can forge a path to success that is not only sustainable but also inspiring. As they embark on this journey, it is essential to remain open to learning, adapting, and evolving. In doing so, they will not only navigate the complexities of the global marketplace but will also thrive, leaving a lasting impact on their industries and communities. The journey is just beginning - let's embrace it together.

Your Path to Streamlined Success

As we draw the curtain on "Streamlining Success: Global Business Services for Human Resources, Digital Marketing, and Management in SMEs," it is vital to take a moment to reflect on the profound insights and transformative strategies we have explored throughout this journey. This book has served as a comprehensive guide, illuminating the pivotal role that Global Business Services (GBS) play in enhancing operational efficiency and strategic positioning for small and medium-sized enterprises (SMEs) in an increasingly competitive global landscape.

In our first chapters, we examined the evolution of GBS, tracing its roots and understanding how it has become an indispensable component of modern business operations. We discussed the importance of GBS in SMEs, highlighting how these services can streamline processes, reduce costs, and ultimately drive growth. The trends shaping the future of GBS are not just theoretical; they are practical realities that every SME must consider as they navigate their unique challenges.

The subsequent chapters delved into specific areas where GBS can revolutionize traditional practices. In human resources, we redefined HR functions within SMEs by leveraging technology to enhance efficiency and effectiveness. The concept of building a global talent pipeline emerged as a crucial strategy for attracting and retaining top talent in a competitive market. By embracing innovative HR practices, SMEs can position themselves as employers of choice, fostering a culture that values diversity and inclusion.

Digital marketing strategies were another focal point of our exploration. We dissected the digital landscape, identifying both opportunities and challenges that SMEs face in this ever-evolving arena. Crafting a winning digital marketing plan requires not only creativity but also a keen understanding of data analytics to measure success through key performance indicators (KPIs). As we navigated through these strategies, it became clear that digital marketing is not merely an option but a necessity for SMEs aiming to thrive in today's marketplace.

Management excellence was another critical theme woven throughout our discussions. We emphasized the role of effective leadership in global operations and explored strategies for fostering a culture of continuous improvement within organizations. The synergy between HR, marketing, and management cannot be overstated; when these functions collaborate seamlessly, they create a powerful engine for driving organizational success.

However, no journey is without its challenges. In Chapter 6, we confronted common pitfalls faced by SMEs when implementing GBS initiatives. Identifying these obstacles is the first step toward overcoming them. We provided actionable strategies for risk management and highlighted the importance of adaptability in operations - qualities that are essential for any SME striving to remain relevant in a rapidly changing environment.

Looking ahead to the future of SMEs in a globalized world, we discussed the imperative to embrace innovation and technology while also prioritizing sustainability and social responsibility. These elements are no longer optional; they are integral to building resilient businesses that can withstand economic fluctuations and societal shifts. Preparing for the next generation of business leaders means instilling values that prioritize ethical practices alongside profitability.

In Chapter 8, we outlined actionable steps for SMEs and startups seeking to implement these insights effectively. Developing a strategic roadmap tailored to your organization's unique needs is crucial for navigating the complexities of modern business landscapes. Building a resilient business model involves not only financial planning but also cultivating an agile mindset that embraces change as an opportunity rather than a threat.

The inspiring success stories shared throughout this book serve as powerful reminders of what is possible when vision meets action. Interviews with SME leaders who have successfully integrated GBS into their operations provide valuable lessons learned from both failures and triumphs. These narratives underscore the power of community and collaboration—elements that can propel any organization toward achieving its goals.

As you embark on your own path to streamlined success, remember that every step taken towards integration and collaboration brings you closer to realizing your aspirations. The journey may be fraught with challenges, but each obstacle presents an opportunity for growth and learning. Embrace this journey with confidence; trust in your ability to adapt and innovate as you move forward.

Now is the time to take charge—develop your strategic roadmap with clarity and purpose, build a resilient business model that can weather storms, and cultivate a network of support that will empower you along the way. Surround yourself with mentors, peers, and resources that inspire you to push boundaries and explore new horizons.

In conclusion, I want to express my heartfelt gratitude for joining me on this exploration of Global Business Services within SMEs. May your endeavors be fruitful, your innovations impactful, and your successes abundant as you forge ahead into a promising future filled with possibilities.

Together, let us embrace change as we strive for excellence in all aspects of our businesses—because streamlined success is not just an end goal; it is an ongoing journey marked by continuous improvement, collaboration, and unwavering commitment to making a difference in our industries.

Sebastian Römischer

www.ingramcontent.com/pod-product-compliance
Lightning Source LLC
Chambersburg PA
CBHW071039240526
45469CB00006BD/2260